SAINT PATRICK

AND THE IRISH

By

Richard Cardinal Cushing

UT COGNOSCANT TE

ST. PAUL EDITIONS

Library of Congress Catalog Card Number: 63—14892

Copyright, © 1979, 1963, by the Daughters of St. Paul

Printed in the U.S.A. by the Daughters of St. Paul
50 St. Paul's Ave., Boston, Ma. 02130

ST. PATRICK'S BREASTPLATE

Christ be my light to illumine and
guide me!
Christ be my shield to cover and
guard me!
Christ be under me, Christ be over
me,
Christ beside me, left and right—
Christ before me, behind me, about
me,
Christ this day within, without
me—
Christ in every heart that thinks
of me—
Christ in every mouth that speaks
to me—
Christ in every eye that sees me—
Christ in every ear that hears me!

CONTENTS

I

THE MAN AND THE LAND

The Man and the Land

More than fifteen hundred years ago there stood before the Court of Tara, in pagan Ireland, one of the greatest missionaries of all times. His fearless eyes glowed with mystic fire that instilled awe and reverence into human hearts. His face was stamped with nobility and strength of character and holiness sublime, yet bore the traces of severest hardships and sternest discipline. An expressive countenance was his, calm with the peace that came from intimate and constant union with Divinity, yet glowing with the fire and beauty that showed a great heart which loved with an all-consuming love the people of Ireland. That missionary was Patrick, the Apostle of Erin.

He was already a great saint, with every human passion quelled by a life of constant prayer, fasting and penance: a saint with a faith that was almost vision, with a burning love of God and an overwhelming longing to bring the souls of the Irish to the feet of Christ.

There at Tara he was starting at last on his life-mission, after years of solemn, prayerful preparation and with a commission and blessing from Christ's Vicar, Pope Celestine, to preach the Gospel in Ireland. Born somewhere in Great Britain in the latter part of the Fourth Century, in his youth Patrick had heard "the call of the Irish"—the people who, in his boyhood days, he had served as a slave. Liberated from bondage, he listened to the eager chorus of many voices pleading for his return to the land of his bondage. "O holy youth, come back to Erin and walk once more among us." Through years of self-mastery the cry was always in his ears, and in his heart a desire irresistible–a desire fulfilled when he stood before the High King at Tara, to start his mission of spreading the sunshine of God's grace over the Irish woods and hills and valleys, and to win the nation's loving and abiding fealty for Christ.

The foundation of his preparation for the apostolate, the background of Patrick's crowded and anguished activity, was prayer. Before he was shanghied, at the age of sixteen, and brought across the Irish Sea, to tend sheep on the hillside, he had been pleasure-loving, neglectful of study, disobedient at home. When he was snatched at sixteen from this life of ease, his nights on the Irish hills were cold and lonely, and cattle-watching, in slavery, was a great indignity to the son of a Roman official. He could have sunk into a state of resentment and rebellion; he could have sulked or despaired; in a dozen ways that a sixteen-year-old boy knows, he could have marked himself as a misfit who should have been left on the shores of the English Channel.

But none of these ways of self-assertion did he adopt, none of these forms of resentment did he employ. Instead, he prayed. And as he prayed, he grew in sanctity. "The love of God came to me more and more," he wrote, "and my faith was strengthened. My spirit was moved so that in a single day

I would say as many as a hundred prayers, and almost as many in the night. And when I was staying in the woods and on the mountain, I would get up for prayer before daylight, through snow, through frost, through rain."

Before Patrick appeared in history as a missionary, priest, bishop, organizer, teacher who could reach the pagan mind and convert it to the truth of Christ; before we meet him as a giant of activity he had already become a giant of spirituality—six years on a mountaintop, alone with God, enriched with later years of prayer and study.

Where in all the writings of the saints, in all literature, can you find an example of more active cooperation with the Holy Spirit? His years of slavery became a long uninterrupted retreat in which his soul developed, year by year, into greater holiness and closer intimacy with God.

Young though Patrick was during this six-year retreat, he understood the force of persecution, the sublimity of humility and their effect upon his friendship with God. "This I know," he wrote at the end of his life, "that before I was humiliated I was like a stone lying in the deep mire. Then He that is mighty came and in His mercy lifted me up, and raised me aloft, and placed me on the top of the wall. Therefore, I ought to cry out aloud and render thanks to the Lord for His great benefits here and in eternity." What a perfect epitomizing of Patrick's humility: a stone lying in the deep mire whom God placed on the top of the wall!

St. Patrick won Ireland and Ireland won Patrick. He confined his apostolate to no special sect or clan or class; he allowed no inter-tribal spleen to interfere with his mission; by his tact, his power of eloquence, his winning ways, his touching love for the people, above all, by his holiness. he won the hearts of serf and king, druid and bard, soldier, hunter and statesman.

It was not required that he would seal his work with his lifeblood. The great, kind-hearted, fiery people of Ireland recognized his goodness and gave a ready ear and reverence to their apostolic messenger. They took him to their hearts; they followed his instruction; they believed his message; they quickly abandoned their idols and learned to worship and love the One True God. They hearkened to the teaching which the Son of God bequeathed to the world. They assimilated the Divine Truths; they lived on them as on the pure air of their mountains. Christianity became part of their very being. Their sons in multitude gave themselves up to the complete service of God and His church. Their daughters bound themselves in communities and took Christ for their spouse. The rich gave abundantly of their wealth to build edifices suitable to divine worship, to provide monasteries for their monks, convents for their nuns and schools at which their youth would imbibe sacred teachings.

Within twenty-five years after his coming, the whole island was Catholic. And the saint, before his death, had consecrated three hundred and fifty bishops, ordained over five thousand priests and built more than seven hundred churches. This was the legacy he left to his people; but a greater legacy was the memory of his saintly life, of his strong faith, and of his perfect trust in God.

All Saint Patrick's sanctity was directed towards one objective: the glory of God achieved by the salvation of men. Therein is to be found the greatest of his virtues, his unquenchable zeal for souls. Listen to his own words:

"I was born of a father who was a decurion (that is, a minor Roman noble), but I sold my nobility, I blush not to state, nor am I sorry. I sold my nobility for the profit of others. In short I am a slave in Christ to a foreign land on account of the ineffable glory of the eternal life which is in Christ, our Lord."

The glory of God, there is the secret of all his praying and suffering as a slave boy. The glory of God, there is the motivating force for all his ar-

A CHURCH BUILT CLOSE TO THE TIME
OF ST. PATRICK, BEFORE 664

duous, weary years of preparation in the monasteries of Gaul. The glory of God, there is the continual incentive that drove him on, an old man of sixty years and more, to evangelize the whole of Ireland. Was there a distant mission to be established? Patrick trod the whole, weary journey unfalteringly. Was there a treacherous chieftain to be braved, or a savage people to be led into the fold? Patrick never hesitated. Did he not write:

"And if I should be worthy I am ready to give up even life most willingly and unhesitatingly for His name's sake." The never-ending road, the foaming torrent, the steep mountainside, could these be barriers to him? Beyond the high ridges of the mountain, on the other bank of the turbulent, roaring waters, at the end of long-extending roads were souls, souls for whom Christ had died, and Patrick must bring them to his Crucified Master.

Nor could the closest human ties bind this holy patriarch. In all the calendar of the saints there is not one who loved his kindred more than did St. Patrick. In writing of his longing to visit again his country and his parents and to gaze once more on the faces of his monastic brethren in Gaul, he cries out from the depths of his heart: "God knows how much I longed to see them." But he would not leave Ireland, lest he should lose any of the children he had begotten in Christ.

Imprisonment, physical assaults, even the shadow of death could not deter him. Calmly he states it: "Daily I am expecting to be slain, or set upon, or reduced to slavery." Yet this is how he faced every threat and every danger: "I beg God to grant me that I may shed my blood with these strangers and captives for His name's sake, even though I should be without burial itself, or that my corpse should most miserably be divided limb from limb among dogs and fierce beasts, or that the birds of the air should devour it." There is St. Patrick. Rather than lose one soul whom he had gained for Christ, he would gladly drain his blood to the last drop though his corpse became the food of scavenging mongrels and the carrion of birds of prey.

II

SUCCESS AND CRITICISM

Success and Criticism

In many respects the events of the fourth and fifth centuries are among the most salient in importance and the most far-reaching in influence of any era in the life of the Church founded by our Divine Savior Jesus Christ. It was in the first quarter of the fourth century, for example, that the Church, in consequence of the Edict of Milan issued by the

27

Emperor Constantine in the year 313, by which toleration was granted to all religions, rose triumphantly from the stygian blackness and the humiliating obscurity of the Roman catacombs. Indeed by the close of that century, due to the official action of the Emperor Theodosius, Christianity had become the formally recognized state religion.

Ecumenical Councils have been described as the nerve centers of Christ's Mystical Body. The first of such Councils convened in the year 325 at Nicaea and, condemning the heresy of Arianism, solemnly proclaimed the consubstantiality of God the Son with God the Father.

That same century witnessed the second Ecumenical Council, which was held at Constantinople in the year 381, and which defined infallibly the divinity of the Holy Spirit.

In the following century likewise two Ecumenical Councils were convoked: that of Ephesus which definitively affirmed the divine maternity of the Blessed Virgin Mary, and that of Chalcedon which proscribed the heretical teaching that there existed in Jesus Christ only one nature.

Few eras in ecclesiastical history can so justifiably boast of so many brilliant luminaries in the firmament of Christianity: in the West, Ambrose and Augustine and Jerome and Hilary and Paulinus and Peter Chrysologus–to mention but a few; and in the East, Athanasius and Cyril of Jerusalem and Cyril of Alexandria and John Chrysostom and Ephraem and the three Cappadocians.

The papacy too was graced with pontiffs of scholarship and renown, holy men and able men, men of action and men of books–popes like "the ornament and glory of Rome", Damasus I in the fourth century, who fixed the canon of the Scripture and fostered Jerome's revision of the translation of the Bible; popes like the sagacious and fearless Leo the Great in the fifth century, one of the most illustrious leaders in the long line of Christ's Vicars, who, armed only with the weapons of the spirit, forced the barbarian Attila to turn back to Mantua.

The era which we are discussing witnessed dire and varied perils for the Church and for all civilization. From beyond the frontiers of the empire, from east of the Rhine and north of the Danube began to pour in the barbarian invaders, oftentimes to plunder and to pillage, but ultimately to transform a western empire that had disintegrated and toppled before them.

Yes, it is indeed no exaggeration to state that the events of the fourth and fifth centuries are among the most salient in importance and the most far-reaching in influence of any era in the life of the Church founded by our Divine Savior Jesus Christ.

To us who live in the twentieth century, and who from this vantage point enjoy the benefit of historical perspective, it seems abundantly clear that no event of the era upon which we are reflecting had more vast and enormous consequences for the Church Universal than the life and the mission of the Apostle of Ireland, St. Patrick.

His was one of the most successful missionary enterprises in human history.

When Patrick's days were over, he saw a whole land evangelized and he alone of all his great contemporaries of the Christian West had the unique privilege of finding a people predominantly pagan on his arrival and leaving them wholly Christian at his death. This amazing transformation was accomplished in thirty years. If, as the Emperor Augustine could say of Rome, "I found it a city of brick and left it a city of marble," Patrick could say before the judgment seat of God, "I found Ireland bound to idolatry and superstition; I left it consecrated forever to Thy Divine Son made Man of Mary and crucified for our salvation."

The conversion of Ireland by St. Patrick has long been considered a unique miracle of grace.

Success and Criticism

True enough, the Hand of God was in it; the complete and thorough change of an entire country from druidic myth to Christian devotion in the space of thirty years, without martyrdom or heresy, is an astounding, if not miraculous event. And Patrick was the first to praise God for it. But we must not forget—and God would want us to remember—the human agent of His grace, the most practical and efficient apostle, after St. Paul, in the history of the Church.

It is easy and natural to think of St. Patrick as a man of such evident charm and sanctity that people rushed to his leadership. He had indeed personal charm and sanctity, but so had Palladius, who preceded him in Ireland and who failed. St. Patrick, however, had a plan, and the means and the will to see that it worked. When he arrived in a town he brought with him a retinue consisting of never less than twenty-four persons, often the number ran to a hundred. The group usually included an assistant bishop, a chaplain, several young men whom Patrick was preparing for the priesthood, a brehon or judge, to advise him on legal matters, builders, masons, smiths, metal-workers, chariot and wagon drivers, a cook, a brewer, and two table attendants. Besides these, there were the sacristan and three embroidery-workers to prepare the linens for the altar, and a psalmist who would be the custodian of the sacred books.

Among the treasures of workmanship left in each church by the artisans who accompanied St. Patrick was a book of the Gospels. Scribes with painstaking care made copies by hand of the sacred books, and the metal-workers, coppersmiths provided the covers. Many of these books were supplied by the monasteries, which sprang up in Ireland soon after St. Patrick brought the Faith to the land and became the citadels of Christian piety, learning, and civilization for the next five centuries. One of those Gospel books, used in the divine service of a Church in Ireland more than a thousand years ago, is the very beautiful *Book of Kells,* a famous example of the Irish art of illumination.

St. Patrick himself examined the possibilities of every district, discovered the local condition for his work, and in general mastered the situation. While the church was under construction he either helped the builders or preached and baptized in the district. He was ready to move on only when the church had been finished, equipped and consecrated, and a permanent pastor, one of his trained disciples, placed in charge. The modern efficiency expert would do well, in many ways, to study the technique of St. Patrick.

32

THE BOOK OF KELLS

Beginning of St. Mark's Gospel

So stupendous was the success of Patrick's missionary apostolate that one may be tempted to overlook the indisputable historical fact that staggering difficulties ceaselessly beset him on every side. No less than a dozen times he was seized and carried off as a prisoner. Once he was sentenced to die. On another occasion he escaped death, only because a faithful and loyal disciple, secretly learning of an attempt to be made upon Patrick's life, deliberately put himself in his master's place. Indeed so enormous and diversified were the hardships which Patrick endured and so uninterrupted and endless the perils to his life, that some of the earlier martyrologies actually speak of him as a martyr.

It was only Patrick's deep interior life, centering about his faith in the presence of the living God within him, that sustained him and encouraged him and inspired him, as he went about, year after year, from one end of Ireland to the other, preaching the Gospel, converting souls, establishing churches, consecrating bishops and ordaining priests.

In the telling of the story of Patrick, early Christian times were as exposed to literary exaggerations as we are. Thus, the character of St. Patrick became distorted beyond all recognition. There were exaggerations and legends already in circulation about him during his lifetime. With the centu-

THE BOOK OF KELLS
Details

ries they were amplified, encrusted and solidified–
and are as false as the physical representation of
Patrick in statuary and illustration.

Patrick was much greater, more wonderful,
more admirable than the stories associated with his
name. Even in his own lifetime St. Patrick, as well
as Patrick the man and missionary, was misunder-
stood, misrepresented, and slandered so that he was
forced to defend himself against his detractors in
Great Britain, in France, and in Ireland itself.

To all this has been added the clamor of dis-
puting scholars, philologists, antiquarians, historians, learned and expert in their field, but who, like
the mythmakers and taletellers, in pursuit of their
ends and their profession have lost the man. They
likewise lost the Saint, for all saints were first men
with all of the strength and the weakness, the turpi-
tude and nobility, to be found intermingled in the
human being. Where then shall we go for the truth?

There are only two great, authentic documents
written by the hand of St. Patrick himself. One is
the *Confessio,* or Confession of St. Patrick, as he
himself referred to it, and the other his *Letter to the
Soldiers of Coroticus.*

"This is my confession before I die," is how
Patrick ends the first work, but it is more than a
mere "confession", it is a testament of his labors,

a self-defense, and a thanksgiving to God conceived on a simultaneously grand and humble scale. Here and there it is enriched with fascinating biographical flashes and glimpses. It is studded with quotations from Scripture. The style is that of a man of action unfamiliar with the tricks of the pen and the skill of good writers. It is often rambling and inconsequent, although the copyists may also be at fault. Certain passages are obscure. They are written by an old man, a hurt and sensitive old man looking back over a long, adventurous, and dedicated life.

The second document from Patrick himself is *The Letter to the Soldiers of Coroticus*. It is a flamingly angry epistle of denunciation and excommunication written to the soldiers of a Welsh chieftain. Coroticus, but against Coroticus himself and meant to be read in his presence, or in the presence of his friends and supporters. It was prompted by the fact that the soldiers of Coroticus–nominally Christians, though there is indication that their ranks consisted of apostates, heathens and adventurers for booty, who reversed the more familiar proceeding by raiding the Irish coast from the British–had come upon a flock of Patrick's newly baptized Christians. They slaughtered many, and sold the rest into slavery to heathen nations.

Imbedded in these two documents is to be found the true personality of a man who, like other great

37

bearers of the message of the Gospels, was not to be
stilled by the crushing weight of the centuries and to
whose achievements the Irish nation and people of
today are a living monument. The apostolic labors
of Patrick, the Gospel he preached, the loyalties he
practiced all reveal him as a great spiritual giant.

His singleness of purpose, his unselfish dedication to the Gospel, his nostalgia for Ireland while
he was away from it, his crusading desire to achieve
its perfection when he was back on its shores–all
these were narrated by Patrick in his *Confession*.

It is evident also from his own writings that his
peaceful conquest of Ireland was never touched
with the least suggestion of exploitation. He must
have drawn heavily upon some missionary funds
upon the continent, for he seems to have personally
financed the whole enterprise in order to win the
people's confidence. He accepted nothing from
them, not even, he wrote, 'laborer's hire." He tells
us that he had a horror of receiving any material
reward for his work, that when pious women gave
him gifts to express their recognition, he returned
them, even when those gifts were cast upon the
altar, preferring to cause a little hurt than to permit
the initiation of a doubtful practice. He served his
co-workers without accepting from them, as he
phrases it himself, "even the price of my shoe".

Success and Criticism

"I did this so as to keep myself detached from all things", he said, "and that I should not, even in the smallest matter, give occasion to the unbelievers to defame or disparage." The greatest sermon he ever preached was his own life. He was "not deterred by cold, not possessed by hunger or thirst, sleeping on a bare stone, with a wet cloak around him, a rock for his pillow . . . enduring great toil."

Certain critics had belittled Patrick's learning and abilities; others had questioned his wisdom and the effectiveness of his apostolic methods. Patrick feared that their criticisms might gravely prejudice the success of his Irish mission. So he penned his apologia, laying bare his very soul, explaining his most intimate motives with the greatest care, even recounting the wonderful favors that God had bestowed upon him. Since the *Confession* was written in his old age, Patrick has given the complete revelation of his soul. What manner of man do we discover in the pages of this vital document? There stands before us a single-minded saint, entirely preoccupied with God, an humble laborer steeped in the deepest lowliness, a prayerful worshipper ceaseless in divine supplication, a dedicated missionary with heart aflame for the salvation of souls.

A single-minded saint, preoccupied entirely with God, he proclaimed publicly God's mercies to him. In the scriptural sense he would confess before men God's works and God's glory. He desired the world to know how wonderfully God had called him and, too, how wonderfully God had prepared him for the task. He would have friend and foe recognize that his entire apostolate was not his own doing but God's. Thus in an early paragraph Patrick puts down the keynote of the *Confession*: "Therefore I cannot conceal, nor is it indeed fitting, the great favors, and the great grace which the Lord has vouchsafed to bestow on me in the land of my captivity. For this is the return we make, that after our chastisement or after our recognition of God we should exalt and proclaim His wondrous ways before every nation which is under heaven." The old apostle then pours forth fervent thanks to God, gratefully enumerating God's many benefits; for helping him in the hour of his trial; for deigning to choose him for the great work of converting the people of Hibernia; for giving him the grace to persevere, to overcome all difficulties, and to leave his country, family and friends; finally for delivering him from slavery, plots and countless dangers Patrick eagerly credits God for his successes: "It was not my grace," he wrote, "but God who put this earnest care into my heart, that I should be one of the hunters or fishermen, who long ago God foretold would come in the last days."

Success and Criticism

Near the end of the *Confession* the venerable saint reiterates his motivation: "I testify in truth and in the joy of my heart, before God and His holy angels that I never had any motive except the Gospel and its promises in ever returning to that nation from which on a former occasion I had escaped with difficulty."

The acid test of St. Patrick's sanctity was his humility. For sanctity is only genuine when it is rooted in an humble heart. Humility permeates every line of the *Confession*. In defense of his mission and in proof of his authority, Patrick was forced to give an accounting of the virtues he had practiced so eminently in God's service and to detail the favors which God had bestowed upon him. A cynical sceptic scrutinizing the lines of this document would search in vain for a single manifestation of pride, conceit, or self-complacency. But on every page he would encounter instances of the deepest humility; he would find the saint ever blaming his failures on his own faults, but ever attributing his successes to the help of Almighty God. Is not this the essence of humility? Why, the very first lines commence:

"I, Patrick, a sinner, am the most uncultivated and the least of all the faithful, and I am held in contempt by many."

St. Patrick and the Irish

Small-minded critics had dismissed Patrick as a mere rustic, as one halting in speech and incapable of writing Latin in the classical style. He did not hesitate to acknowledge his literary and scholastic shortcomings, frankly stating: "Whence today I am ashamed and exceedingly afraid to expose my want of skill, because, not being learned, I am unable to express myself in a few words." We might well wonder why these fault-finding individuals, confronted by the patent achievements of the veteran missionary, could make no allowances for a man who had spent six years of his youth as a swineherd in a foreign land and who had been unable to begin his priestly studies until well advanced in years. But the humble Patrick explains forthrightly his deficiencies: "Seeing that I am not learned like others, who in the best style have drunk in both laws and sacred letters in equal perfection, and who from their infancy never changed their mother tongue, but were rather making it always perfect. My speech, however, and my style were changed into the tongue of the strangers, as it can be easily perceived in the flow of my writings."

Some of his critics had alleged that Patrick had unduly thrust himself forward into his mission, ig- noring his lack of knowledge and his slowness of tongue. To these disparagers he replied: "Whence I, at first a rustic and an exile, unlearned surely as

one who knows not how to provide for the future."
But he hastens to add, ever grateful to God: "Yet
this I do most certainly know that before I was hum-
bled I was like a stone which lies in the deep mire
and He that is mighty came and in His mercy lifted
me up and placed me on the top of the wall. Therefore, I ought to cry out aloud and render thanks to
the Lord for His great benefits here and in eternity."

To one who reads superficially the life of
St. Patrick it might appear that he was simply a
man of extraordinary action and nothing more–
enthusiastic, eager, intent, constantly simmering
with the restlessness to carry the Gospel of Christ
to the ends of the land that had been committed to
his missionary care. But the more discerning student
who penetrates to the reality beneath the persistent
activity of Patrick's career will come to the
knowledge of a soul deeply immersed in the things
of the spirit. The striking achievements of his her-
culean toil no one can deny. But like every true
saint, Patrick realized that what God demanded of
him primarily and essentially was not his gifts, but
himself, not his success but his soul. Patrick was
profoundly cognizant of the truth which St. John
of the Cross was to express so concisely centuries later in *The Spiritual Canticle*: "An instant of
pure love is more precious in the eyes of God and

43

of the soul, and more profitable to the Church, than all other good works put together, although it may seem as if nothing were done."

The life of every saint may be described in terms of heroic virtue—all virtue. Yet it sometimes happens that some special aspect of a soul's nobility shines forth with such dazzling brilliance that it is ascribed to the saint as altogether characteristic. May we not say that such is true of Patrick's faith in the living God? Fundamental to every virtue that he possessed in the depths of his soul was this living, throbbing, absorbing sense of the all-pervading presence of God.

It was this sense of the presence of God that informed his profound interior life, and it was this sense of the presence of God that motivated his extraordinary apostolic life. In the depths of his own soul he strove day in and day out for ever closer union with God Who dwelt within him; and the ultimate goal of all his tireless missionary activity was the service of God in the souls of others.

Even the most cursory perusal of the life of St. Patrick cannot fail to bring to light the myriad sorrows and trials which pervaded it from start to finish. Consider, for instance, the torment and torture of the crushing spiritual crisis which he underwent when he was summarily rejected, and the ill-

LOUGH DERGH
ST. PATRICK'S PURGATORY

fated Palladius chosen to head the first mission to Ireland–a crisis so soul-searing that even in his old age the harrowing memory of it could not be obliterated.

Consider the continual and unremitting opposition that dogged his steps throughout his entire missionary career. Nor was its origin in the druid element alone. Though in Ireland he was "venerated as an angel"–as his companion Secundinus informs us–yet in Britain, there were those who through misunderstanding or envy or malice, hesitated not to accuse him of selfishness and ambition and want of training and defect of education.

Truly it was only a man of deep interior spirituality who could have borne the weight of such crosses.

Patrick's spirituality had been nurtured in the silence and solitude of the Antrim hills where, as he tended his master's flocks for six long years, he completed his novitiate of preparation for his future apostolate. It was there that he cultivated that spirit of contemplation, of austerity and of self-denial, so strikingly manifested all the days of his life–a spirit that prompted him, even in the most active hours of his apostolate, to withdraw from time to time to the seclusion of Lough Dergh or to the summit of what we now call Croagh Patrick, in order to devote himself to prayer and to penance.

Success and Criticism

In the midst of his apostolic laborings the lips of the apostle were ever moving in frequent prayer; even his rest and sleeping time he shared with holy supplication. Then there were the occasions when, withdrawing to remote places, he devoted entire nights and days, and even weeks, to solitary communion with God. Just such a long vigil of prayer and penance did he spend on that lonely island in desolate Lough Dergh, or again on the bare summit of Croagh Patrick storm-swept by the gales that howled in from the North Atlantic. Would you gauge the intensity of Patrick's praying? Then read aloud the passionate invocations of the *Breastplate* and try to feel, even if remotely, the fervor of his calling upon God, and the angels and the saints to be beside him in his battling with the powers of darkness. He had one weapon to conquer idolatry, he had one means of strengthening Erin in her new-found Faith, and he had one legacy for his Irish children—prayer.

Witness his mighty prayer at Tara:

At Tara in this awful hour, *I call upon the Trinity*:
Glory to Him Who reigneth in power,
The God of elements, Father and Son,
The Holy Spirit, Which Three are but One
Omnipotent, Eternal Deity.

St. Patrick and the Irish

This day I call upon the Lord.
On Christ, Whose might shall be my sword:—
the might of His Birth and His Baptism;
the might of His Life and of His Death;
the might by which He rose and reigns;
the might by which He comes to judge.

This day I call upon the Lord,
to make me *strong with seraph's power;*
to make me *share* in angel's *love;*
in all the *merits* of the saints;
in all the *prayers* of patriarchs;
in preaching by apostles done;
in *glory* by the martyrs won;
confessors' *faith* and virgins' *hope*—
in all the *charity* of righteous men.

This day I call upon the Lord,
May God's Own life my life preserve;
May God's Own wisdom be my guide;
May God's Own vision be my sight;
May God's Own ear my hearing be;
May God's Own word bespeak my thoughts;
God's arm bring down my foes to naught;
God's hand defend me from all hurt:
     —against the wiles of demon craft
     —against the snares of evil men
     —against whate'er might cause my fall.

48

Success and Criticism

Christ be my light to illumine and guide me!
Christ be my shield to cover and guard me!
Christ be under me, Christ be over me,
Christ beside me, left and right–
Christ before me, behind me, about me,
Christ this day within, without me–
Christ in every heart that thinks of me–
Christ in every mouth that speaks to me–
Christ in every eye that sees me–
Christ in every ear that hears me!

This day I call upon the Lord,
    upon the Holy Trinity,
    upon the source of our salvation,
to bless our *homes,* our *lands,* our *race*–
to grant us *peace*–His *mercy*–and His *grace.*
                Amen.

III

PATRIARCH AND APOSTLE

Patriarch and Apostle

"And the Lord said to Abraham: 'Go forth out of thy country, and from thy kindred, and out of thy father's house, and come into the land which I will show thee. And I will make thee a great nation, and I will bless thee, and magnify thy name, and thou shalt be blessed." (Genesis 12:1, 2.)

53

With these words the Lord called Abraham to
His service. He responded with complete obedience
and God, true to His promise, made him the
Patriarch of the Hebrew people. Many centuries
later, in the New Dispensation, the Lord called
Patrick to His service. He responded with an obedience like unto Abraham's, and God made St. Patrick the Patriarch of the Irish race.

A patriarch is the founder of a people; he is
their first religious leader, and finally he is the principal molder of their destiny. Certainly St. Patrick
has been all these in the fullest measure. When he
brought Irish pagans into the fold of Christ
by an almost total conversion, a conversion as
thorough as it was widespread, he founded a new
people, a Catholic people, whose distinguishing
characteristic in the subsequent fifteen centuries
was to be unswerving, yea, even passionate loyalty
to the Catholic Church and to its head, Christ's
earthly Vicar, the Pope of Rome.

How could Patrick have done otherwise? He
came as the accredited successor of St. Palladius,
the first delegate of Pope St. Celestine "to those of
the Irish believing in Christ". He came consecrated
as a bishop and commissioned, if not personally by
St. Celestine, at least by that pope's legate and most
ardent champion, St. Germanus of Auxerre. Fur-

thermore, all the evidence and all the traditions of the early Irish church prove that St. Patrick founded a church that was part of the universal Church and that it acknowledged the Pope as its visible head. If proof is needed, there is the ancient Canon of St. Patrick which prescribed recourse to the Apostolic See in questions of great difficulty. The authenticity of this Canon is accepted by modern critics. There is the *Hymn of St. Secundinus*—a disciple of St. Patrick who died before him—with its praise of St. Patrick's loyalty to Peter's successor. And there is the testimony of St. Columban, the greatest of all Irish missionary monks, who certainly knew the ancient Irish Church if anyone did. He has several statements of unequivocal acceptance of the Papal supremacy. But he climaxes them all by his emphatic declaration that all the Irish had received nothing but the apostolic faith, that amongst them there had never been a heretic nor a schismatic, and that they had held unstained and unshaken the Catholic Faith as it had first been transmitted to them from the Popes, the successors of St. Peter.

When Patrick, the patriarch, converted Ireland into a Catholic nation he became its greatest benefactor, for he bestowed upon it its most priceless possession, its Faith. Whatever goodness and nobility are found in Irish hearts they spring from, or at least have been sanctified by that Faith: that faith has been the unfailing strength that sustained the Irish people through the many sorrow-filled centuries that mark their history. It has brought the men and women of Erin, the great and the small, the rich and the poor, the learned and the unlettered to the eternal, loving embrace of the Lord and Mary, His mother. How grateful they ought to be to their holy patriarch because he dug so deep and laid so strongly the foundations of that Faith in the hearts of the children of the Gael that neither oppression nor slavery, destitution nor famine, no, not even death nor wholesale massacre has been fierce enough to rob the Irish of that pearl of great price.

A patriarch is also the first religious leader of his people, directing them, principally by his own example, in the love and service of God. St. Patrick was such a religious leader because his holy example has shown all generations of the Irish how to love and serve God.

A patriarch is the principal molder of the destiny of his people. He sets for them their course in time and for eternity. He influences all the subsequent generations through their memory of his counsel and example. The history of his people is to be written from the adherence of their descendents to his ideal. St. Patrick, unquestionably, is the prin-

CROSS OF SAINTS
PATRICK AND COLUMBANUS

cipal molder of the destiny of the Irish people. When he gave them their Faith he set for them their ultimate goal on this earth and in heaven. By his own virtues, his preoccupation with God, his humility, his prayerfulness and his zeal for men's souls, he offered them the sure means of achieving their final purpose. That his influence has remained paramount with all the subsequent generations is the most outstanding and recurring fact in the history of the Irish people.

God promised Abraham in reward for his service that He would make him the patriarch of the Hebrew people, and that He would cause him to be blessed by them. God in rewarding Patrick's service made him the patriarch of the Irish people and caused him to be blessed by them. Fifteen hundred years have passed since this holy patriarch completed his earthly service of God. The Irish people have blessed St. Patrick through every one of those fifteen centuries. They have loved him with a personal affection that has increased in its warmth with the passing of time. They have blessed him by their faithful loyalty to the Catholic Church, which was his heritage for them. They have blessed him by engraving in their hearts and copying in their lives his virtues of preoccupation with God, humility, prayerfulness and zeal for the glory of God through the salvation of men.

Patriarch and Apostle

The Jews think of Abraham as the "lofty
Father" of their tribes; such is the popular interpre-
tation of his very name. The Irish see in Patrick the
Father of all their scattered flock; the popular ob-
servance of his feast all around the globe keeps the
Irish, wherever they may be, a single family. Abraham is the physical progenitor of his people, but his
historic importance derives from the fact that he is
the starting-point of the Old Testament. Patrick is
the spiritual father of his people because his preaching is the starting-point of their knowledge of the
New Testament. The Jews were wont to speak of
God as the God of Abraham; it is no exaggeration
to say that the Irish think of their God as the God
of Patrick.

Abraham was made mighty by his *faith;* of
him the Scriptures say simply: *Abraham believed
God...*, and so powerful was that belief that Abraham would not hesitate to see his own son die rather
than repudiate his faith in God. Abraham's unique
faith in God became, for the Jews, the pledge of
their privileges as the Chosen People. Patrick made
faith, unqualified and indestructible, the supreme
virtue in the thought of his people; it is proverbial
that the devout Irishman would prefer to suffer any
tragedy rather than deny the faith of Patrick. Such
fidelity has been, for the Irish, the title to the unique

honor they claim among the nations of Christendom as a people who have never produced a heresy.

To be the seed of Abraham and the children of Abraham, to do the work of Abraham, to keep the faith of Abraham, to be justified with the faithful Abraham–no Old Testament saint could imagine a greater glory. To be the sons of St. Patrick, to be numbered forever among those justified with the faithful Patrick–no devout among the Irish could know a greater consolation.

St. Patrick can be thought of in terms of other scriptural parallels. I think of him in terms of his resemblance to Moses, who became God's pioneer and prophet, the Lawgiver of a people destined to illumine and to edify all the world with the doctrine that Moses preached to them, even as the sons and daughters of Old Ireland have been a people scattered throughout the world to preach the Faith of Patrick. Patrick, as their Lawgiver, might well be called the Moses of the Irish people. Even the physical features attributed to Moses, the majesty of his bearing, make one think of the imposing statues by which people represent and recall the heroic St. Patrick.

If we go from the Hebrew patriarch to the Apostle of the Gentiles we find numerous episodes in the lives of Paul and Patrick which are striking in their similarity. Both were men who had

worn chains and were therefore passionately devoted to freedom; Paul wore the chains of a prisoner, Patrick had known those of a slave. Both used
their freedom to enslave themselves as the prisoners
of the Lord to preach the truth by which men are
made free.

Both responded with the total gift of themselves to the call from peoples who needed the
Gospel that both preached. Paul heard a voice in
the night which beseeched him: *Come over into
Macedonia, and help us!* Patrick also experienced
the call of voices, the voices of the ancient Irish
who called out for the help of his preaching. St. Patrick writes: "And again after a few years I was in
Britain with my people . . . and there I saw in the
night the vision of a man . . . with countless letters
. . . (and) the opening words were 'the voice of the
Irish' . . . and I thought that at the same moment I
heard their voice: 'We ask thee, boy, come and walk
among us once more.' . . . Thanks be to God, after
many years the Lord gave to them according to
their cry!"

Both St. Paul and St. Patrick preached to pagans the Christian Gospel, and the Faith revealed
in and by Jesus Christ; both converted to Christ
whole peoples, high born and low, and both com-
municated to their converts their own missionary
spirit.

"In journeys often, in perils from floods, in
perils from the Gentiles, in perils in the wilderness,
in labor and hardship, in hunger and thirst, in fast-
ings often, in cold and nakedness . . . " and besides
all these there was the care of all the Christian Communities he founded. This description of limitless
zeal comes from St. Paul's Second Epistle to the
Corinthians. It could have come also from the pen
of the Apostle of Ireland. Scarcely any part of Ireland is without its Crosspatrick. Back and forth he
traveled converting the pagan, erecting churches,
founding monasteries, educating priests, establishing
religious orders and then revisiting the people in all
places where he had preached the word of the Lord.

Both used every device of reason and of rhetoric, every gift of human ingenuity and of divine
grace to win the souls of which they became the
Fathers in Christ: Paul on Mars Hill and in the
Areopagus, preaching to the pagan Athenians; Patrick on the Rock of Cashel preaching to the Gaels;
Paul boldly appearing before rulers of Greece and
Rome, Patrick before the pagan Irish kings; Paul
breaking up the images of Diana of the Ephesians,
Patrick putting out the pagan fire of Baal on Tara—
how many and how dramatic are the parallels between these two mighty men of God!

Both are Catholic in their creed, their vision
and their influence. Both are Roman to the core.

Patriarch and Apostle

St. Paul is forever linked with Peter in the destiny which gave the Church in Rome two such princely founders and enriched the very soil of Rome with the blood of Apostles so glorious. St. Patrick forever linked the Church in Ireland with the Roman See, reminding his people that just as they were Christians, so they must also be Romans.

We might also compare the extraordinary fortitude of these two apostles, their inexhaustible energy, their perfect faith. At the end of their ministry, when the zeal of their Father's house had consumed them, St. Paul wrote his epitaph:–"I have fought the good fight"; St. Patrick did the same when he wrote just prior to his death:–"I can confidently offer Him my soul as a living sacrifice. . . ."

St. Patrick and St. Paul! How easily and how justly we associate the names, the memories, the works of the Apostle of Ireland and the Apostle to the Gentiles!

Both exemplify and enrich the meaning of the title that both bear, the magnificent title "Apostle." The spiritual influence of both has dominated the centuries.

"Their sound has gone forth into all the earth: and their words unto the ends of the world." This text, proper to the Apostles, is deservedly applied to St. Patrick, for he takes his place beside the greatest and most glorious of the Apostles.

IV

THE SONS AND DAUGHTERS OF PATRICK

The Sons and Daughters
of Patrick

The predominant influence of Patrick over the Irish is manifested first by the ardent affection with which they have loved him through all the centuries. Their attachment has been unique by its very intensity, for they have been so devoted to St. Patrick that they have placed him in their affection above all other saints, save only the Blessed Mother of

God and St. Peter, Bishop of Rome. And their attachment has been as warm-hearted as it has been strong. They have revered his memory, they have ever treasured his example, and always they have loved him from the fullness of their hearts. He has left his mark upon the people and upon the land, and is one of those "living" saints whose vibrations still echo after fifteen centuries.

Whence, it may be asked, the influence of St. Patrick? How comes it that a stranger is so lovingly enshrined in the hearts of the people of a land where he once lived and toiled as a slave? No doubt it was partly due to his own character and partly to that of the people he turned to Christ. Devotion of this kind argues great worth in both parties, the saint and his people. The laborer and the soil were matched. The reaper was strong and the harvest was ripe. Saints are God's agents in doing God's work, but the message they carry must be freely received. God equips His messengers, with gifts and graces. He also prepares the people to receive them. Both must respond to God's call. The fact is that we may ourselves be heaped high with God's grace –and yet be lost because of our willful blindness. Both the potential saints and the people of the saints may fall away. Lucifer and Adam were holy, but they lapsed from grace.

68

The Sons and Daughters of Patrick

The duty of a saint, as of all, is to cultivate personal holiness first before attempting to raise others to the heights of grace. This is what St. Patrick did. All through life, he perfected himself, and he strove to lift up the Irish people toward his own moral level. In other words, he did God's work in his own soul and then God's work, through him, was done in the souls of those who came within his influence.

It is often said that certain institutions are the lengthened shadows of the men who shaped them. So in its most ennobled traits the Irish nation is the lengthened shadow of St. Patrick. The most exalted elements of the Irish spirit reflect with faithful exactness the great characteristics of their saint.

The predominant influence of Patrick is manifested by the constant adherence of the succeeding generations to his ideals: loyalty to the Church, preoccupation with God, humility of heart, prayerfulness, penance, and missionary zeal. In their adherence to St. Patrick's legacy of the Catholic Faith his Irish children have copied the dauntless courage of their venerable father. For almost two centuries they suffered the fierce savageries of the Norse pagans. Later for three centuries more they endured the genocidal massacres of the Elizabethans, the vast despoliations of the Stuart planters, the bloody butcherings of the Cromwellians and the total obliterations of the Georgians. Yet through all these dark centuries the Irish clung with passionate loyalty to the Holy See, offering to the Vicar of Christ the holy homage of a martyred nation. No wonder that the Popes time and time again have saluted the children of Patrick as their ever faithful Irish people.

Historians often meditate on the qualities of States, the forms of their greatness and the causes of these triumphs in the lives of nations. The passage of the centuries places all in proper perspective and proves that national success is never to be measured by commercial greatness, by extent of territory or by the subjugation of peoples. These may dazzle the judgment of those whose horizon is narrowed within the confines of a generation or two, but in ultimate terms they rarely prove abiding nobility. A nation, no less than an individual, cannot find true greatness in material acquisitions, but must attain it by righteousness of thought and action.

History is full of the mystery of nations which attained worldly greatness and yet vanished, leaving no trace of a name behind them. This mystery meets the traveler in the buried cities of the forest of Yucatan; it astounds him among African savages and on Asiatic hillsides.

History stores up no less the lesson that whatever the memory of deeds left behind it, the nation which barters its soul for conquest or for power is a nation doomed.

Ireland, despite all her poverty, penury and persecution, has survived because she lived for eternity not time–for the spiritual, not the temporal. She recognized the Savior of men when He came to her, and has ever since been faithful to Him.

Her total acceptance of Christianity and her loyalty to its credo ranks as the outstanding characteristic of Patrick's achievement. Whereas other pagan lands martyred the first missionaries of Christianity or submitted slowly and painfully to the yoke of Christ, Ireland looked upon the Cross and recognized the face of Him who is the Way, the Truth, and the Light of the World. In that full acceptance of the supernatural we find the key of her long history and a powerful answer to many of the evils she has suffered. She was sealed from the beginning to two loyalties–love of the ancient faith and love of the soil which Patrick consecrated by his labors, his mysticism, his miracles, and his vision of the role of pain in the Christian economy of salvation.

The close imitation of St. Patrick's preoccupation with God almost immediately covered Erin with monasteries and crowded them with a veritable host of saints. These holy sons and daughters of the Gael reproduced in their own lives the worship,

71

the prayers and the penances of their father St. Patrick. They earned for their motherland her most glorious title, "the Isle of Saints." Columbkille, Enda and Brendan, Bridget, Ita and Attracta—why, we are calling the role of the national heroes and heroines of Ireland.

There is no such thing as Irish Catholicism in the sense that Catholicism can be divided into various kinds essentially different from one another. Catholicism is one and universal; every school boy knows how and why this must be so. But while there is no such thing as Irish Catholicism, there is such a thing as an Irish Saint. There is an Irish genius in Catholicism as there is a French genius in Catholicism. There is an Irish way of living out the universal Faith, just as there is a German way, an Italian way and an Oriental way.

None of these different "ways" is out of order so long as it remains in Communion with the universal ways of Rome and contributes to the unified life of the Church. The Lord knows that the "Irish way" has always remained in communion with Rome and helped to nourish the life of the world-wide Church!

And so, although there is no such thing as "national Catholicism," still the saints of any nation are most typical of the highest and best aspects of the national character. There is no one more Catholic in

MONASTERY ON SKELLING MICHAEL (KERRY)
Top: a stone hut; bottom: general view

English history than St. Thomas More; neither is there any one more English. There is no one more Catholic in the history of France than St. Joan of Arc; there is also no one more French. There is no one more Irish than St. Patrick, whatever his national origin; there is no one more Catholic or more Roman.

What are the typically Irish aspects of Patrick's personal Catholicism?

You find them echoed in certain phrases and reflected in certain deeds which come down to us in the history and the legends of the Saints. The phrase, for example, with which he himself described the sublime confidence with which, as a runaway slave, he clambered abroad an unknown ship to sail with strangers to a destiny completely unrevealed. He tells us that he cast himself into the hands of God Almighty, having learned as he said, "that God can be trusted utterly." It is a typically Irish conviction.

His singleness of purpose, his nostalgia for Ireland while he was away from it; his crusading desire to achieve its perfection when he was back on its shores; all these are very Irish. But above all, I like to believe, the unselfish dedication of his priestly service of the people stamps him as the ideal Irish priest and has, please God, influenced the idealism of priests of Irish blood down to this day.

74

The Sons and Daughters of Patrick

As the characteristic virtue of St. Patrick is his
ardent zeal for the salvation of men's souls, so the
missionary ideal is the paramount one in his legacy.
The response of the early generations to this missionary ideal constitutes one of the most glorious
achievements of the Irish race. For three hundred
years an army of Irish monks left their beloved Erin
to spend the rest of their lives, and to risk them too,
in bringing the heathen nations of Europe into the
fold of Jesus. Always they kept before their vision
the example of St. Patrick in his conversion of their
own ancestors.

Thus inspired they trudged the wearisome flat
lands of Northern Europe, they toiled up and over
the rugged heights of the Alps, they crossed the
streams of the Rhine and the Danube, they plunged
into the dark, primeval forests of Germany in their
tireless search for souls. Wherever they went they
built their monasteries to be the centers of conversion, of sanctity and of learning. Only the infinite
God could count the number of the souls brought
to His love and worship by these wanderers for
Christ. Columbkille and Aidan, Columban and Gall,
Kilian and Virgilius, Fiachra, Fursey and Livinius—
these are but the captians in that missionary army
of Irish monks, who are the golden glory of Erin,
and of Europe too.

75

Over the centuries, the spirit of Patrick's zeal and Patrick's faith in the living God have never ceased to enkindle in the hearts of Irish missionaries the insatiable passion to evangelize the world. It is a matter of no flowery rhetoric but of sober fact that, while Ireland itself was being dotted with monasteries that became centers of sanctity and learning, in carrying the "Good News" all over continental Europe Columbanus and Columbkille and Kilian and Aidan and Gall and numberless others were responsible for the saving of Western civilization for future ages.

History witnesses to the fact that the Irish missionaries passed through England to northern France and the Netherlands, across the Gaulish sea and by the Loire to middle France; by the Rhine and the way of Luxeuil they entered Switzerland; and eastward they reached out to the Elbe and the Danube, sending missionaries to Old Saxony, Thuringia, Bavaria, Salzburg and Carinthia; and southwards they crossed the Alps into Italy, to Lucca, Fiesole, Rome, the hills of Naples, and Tarentum. . . . Europe itself was too narrow for their ardor, and they journeyed to Jerusalem, settled in Carthage, and sailed to the discovery of Iceland.

In the sailor-missionary, St. Brendan, whose exploits may have brought him into the waters of

ST. COLUMBANUS

our own New England Coast, we see the typical Irish hunger to cross the seas for the sake of the Kingdom, the characteristic audacity of the Irish missionary genius. No people have understood better than the Irish that word of Jesus: "Every one who hath left father or mother or sister or lands, for My sake shall receive a hundredfold." St. Brendan typifies the Irish response to this evangelical challenge.

A voyage of exploration had many attractions for one of Brendan's spirit. It appealed to that virtue of daring he had shown even as a child in the cave, and it held to the alluring prospect of that perfect contemplation possible in a ship at sea. But even stronger reasons impelled him. The early Celtic peoples had an immortal belief in the existence of a fair world beyond the rim of the western ocean. Bearing a variety of names, this island shone in the amber light of romance, reflecting the desires of the different races.

Even in Christian times there was a tradition current along the western seaboard of Ireland that the "Land of Promise" could be seen every seventh year. Brendan could not remain wholly indifferent to such tales. It seems however that his greatest incentive came from a brother monk who had been a navigator credited with western voyages. Having heard this monk's account of his travels, Brendan withdrew to his cell on Brandon Hill. There, for three days, he fasted and prayed for guidance–alone, with the ocean beneath him rolling outward to the alluring west. It was an unequal struggle–and the ocean won.

At the end of the vigil Brendan announced his decision to sail and ordered three boats to be built. A crew of sixty were selected, provisions were gathered, and the day named. Then, with a courage that equalled his faith, he sailed from the Kerry bay that still bears his name and disappeared into romance and mist.

For years thereafter Brendan sailed the Western oceans. What lands did he visit? We do not know. Did he reach the North American Continent, visiting as some say, the Virginia Capes, the Floridas and even Mexico? I cannot say. The only thing I know is this: wherever an Irish nun has brought healing or hope at the ends of the Pacific; wherever an Irish priest has brought Faith beyond the Capes of South Africa and along the coast of Asia; in whatever corner of the world the Catholic Gospel has been heard with an Irish accent,–there the spirit of St. Brendan, navigator and missionary, is still a-voyaging. His influence, Catholic and Irish, still lives to this day.

St. Patrick and the Irish

The monks who went from Ireland in the days of St. Columba, and later Columbanus, brought the Faith back to whole areas of Germany, Gaul, Italy and the East. They did not go as chaplains accompanying military chieftains or political conquerors. Their sole weapons were meekness and humility with which, in the faithful pattern of St. Patrick, they preached the Gospel to rude peoples whose refined descendents remember them still for the meekness and clemency of their ways.

Meekness and humility—they pervaded Patrick's preaching. And these qualities, so marked in the man and his writing, entered Irish Catholicism with the preaching and influence of Patrick.

This typical characteristic of the Irish spiritual tradition is mirrored in the story of St. Columbkille, sometimes hailed as the supreme type of Irish genius. He was an administrator, a diplomat and a born leader. He was, of course, a saint. But it is his meekness and humility which stamp him with the authentic seal of characteristic Irish spirituality.

His mighty missionary enterprise did not begin as a heroic response to a glorious call from God; neither was it launched as a campaign conceived in over-powering ambition to accomplish a resounding victory for the Church. It began as a quiet man's effort to atone for an injustice, to repair by kindness

"ST. COLUMBANUS' HOUSE", KELLS
(the doorway is modern)

damage done in battle. His work, conceived in a spirit of humble reconciliation, began in suffering and in sacrifice. It eventually bore its fruit in a great spiritual harvest. All the historic accomplishments of Columbkille, his chain of monastic foundations and his unique record of administration, began with the humble decision of a peace-loving man to devote himself as best he could, to a work of reconciliation, not of reform and least of all, of revolution.

St. Bridget, daughter of kings and bride of Christ, Ireland's noblest woman, was no less humble. When as many as thirty convents were under her rule, she herself still rose early and, like Patrick, attended to herding sheep.

In an ancient book it is written: "For everything Bridget asked, the Lord granted at once. For this was her desire: to satisfy the poor; to relieve every misery. Never was anyone more bashful, modest, gentle, meek and humble. . . . Innocent, prayerful, patient, glad in God's Commandments, firm, humble, forgiving, loving . . . a consecrated casket for holding Christ's Body and Blood."

It would be a holy joy to dwell on the deeds of other ancient Irish saints: St. Columbanus, civilizer and restorer, St. Malachy, prelate and prophet, St. Laurence O'Toole, good and just man who died in exile as so many Irishmen have done. But come across the centuries to Blessed Oliver Plunket. °

° In 1975, Oliver Plunket was canonized by Pope Paul VI.

This great martyr-bishop represents the typical qualities of the Irish-Catholic at their heroic best. He grew up to manhood at a time when Ireland was most given over to the forces of destruction; no one could understand better than he the special meaning that the Irish give the word "the trouble" as applied to certain moments of their history. He summed up within his single person the qualities of all the great Irishmen of his century; the nobility of the O'Neills and the Roes; the scholarship of Colgan, Keating and Luke Wadding; the genius in administration and the zeal in reform of the 17th century Irish prelates; the constancy in exile and fidelity in suffering of so many of the Irish in his century. And all these he crowned with martyrdom.

It is difficult to tell where lie the more powerful arguments for his sanctity: whether it be among the magnificent deeds of his life as a pontiff and confessor, or whether it be in the circumstances of his death as a martyr. All are characterized by magnificent Catholicism, Catholicism with a bit of the brogue of the Irishmen.

As a Christian, Blessed Plunket was kindly and considerate. He was humble in his great learning. He was assiduous in the fulfillment of the duties of his state in life. He was filled with a holy peace and he saw all events of life in a completely spiritual perspective. Few men in history have accepted injustice and even a brutally unjust death with such magnificent dignity and devout resignation.

The manner of his so-called trial, the prejudiced charge to the jury, the evil temper of the times, all these made the verdict against him inevitable. But he waited serenely for the cruel sentence which only a miracle could avert. The President of the Court charged the jury: "Gentlemen of the jury, look you here, Mr. Plunket here is indicted of high treason; and it is for conspiring the King's death, and endeavoring to bring the French army into Ireland to invade that kingdom and establish therein the Roman religion. If you believe these witnesses that have attested these things against him, you must find him guilty. It is pretty strong evidence, and the prisoner does not say anything against it but that his witnesses are not yet come over."

From the dock, the grave voice of the prisoner replied, "I can say nothing to it but give my protestation that there is not one word of this said against me true, but all plain romance. I never had any communication with any French minister, Cardinal or other."

The jury took a quarter of an hour to bring in their verdict. It was "Guilty." A week later the prisoner was brought to the bar to receive sentence. He knew the savage formula by heart and was calm. The world knows it, and shudders–hanged, drawn, disembowelled, quartered. "Deo gratias!" was the exultant cry. It was the martyr's crown for which he had long prayed!

He was a martyr for his faith. So far as we may use the word, he was also a martyr for Ireland. But his love for Ireland, it must be noted, did not make him the enemy of any other land. On the contrary, Blessed Plunket exemplifies the truly Catholic spirit in which differences between nations must always be resolved no matter what the previous history of injustice or of bitterness on either side.

Blessed Plunket was put to death by the English. He must have been painfully aware, however, that imperfection was by no means limited to members of the nation which had persecuted his people and which had sentenced him to death. He had also been sorely vexed by disloyalties within his own flock and he had tasted, as every leader must, the sour wine of perfidy and intrigue among his own. For all that, they *were* his own and he loved them passionately and served them without cease. In his will he could boast, in homely, touching language: "I stuck to my care and my districts until death!"

Ireland was much in his thoughts in the harassed last hours of his life, even those in Ireland who had kept silent when he needed defense and who seemed to fail him in his hour of need.

And by the same token, he was preserved by his personal sanctity from falling victim to any intemperance in his attitude toward the enemy nation. The English Catholics, at least, had stood by him through all his difficulties, giving him friendship, money and sympathy. He could not entirely hate a nation which included so many devout and generous personal friends. His last will and testament includes a touching tribute to these good people. It is worth remembering, because it reflects again the spirit in which we must all approach partisan differences. He wrote: "The English Catholics here were most charitable to me. They spared neither money nor gold to relieve me, and in my trial did all for me that my brother would do."

One of these Catholic English, a convert to the Faith, a Benedictine monk and a fellow-prisoner became the special friend of Blessed Oliver. They were separated by the walls of their prison cells, but they corresponded in the last days of Plunket's life. In one of his letters Blessed Oliver wrote to Dom Croker: "Being the first of my countrymen to suffer here, I desire to lead the way to others; and it is right I should strengthen by my example those in Ireland whom I have so often exhorted by word of mouth."

The death that lay before him, the detail of its horrors, he prayed over and accepted so often in spirit that by God's grace he could write "compared to the death of the Cross that of Tyburn, as I hear the description of it, is but a flea biting." Easily, as only a man can whose natural courage is supernaturally informed, he writes in the same tone to his nephew Michael Plunket at the Irish College: "I expect daily to be brought to the place of execution, where my bowels are to be cut out and burned before my face and then my head to be cut off, etc., which death I embrace willingly. I expected yesterday to be brought to execution, but finding I am not to be brought to it until Friday or Saturday, I thought fit to write you these few lines."

On the appointed day, July 1, 1781, he was drawn at the horse's tail from Newgate through London, the long two miles or more by which so many had already gone to their victory and crown. Of all that glorious band he was to be the last, and of them all he was the only bishop, for the one other bishop martyred in England had suffered on Tower Hill. At Tyburn, before an immense crowd, he preached his last sermon, prayed his last prayer, calling on Our Lady and the Saints to aid him. Then the Law had its way.

Blessed Oliver Plunket taught the lessons of fortitude and heroic resistance, clemency, Christian

forebearance and flaming charity. Father Croker
watched from the prison windows for the last sight
of him as he was executed. With Croker were other
priests and laymen, all English, sentenced to death
by the same spirit of injustice which had doomed
Blessed Plunket. Croker described the end as fol-
lows: "I neither can nor dare undertake to describe
the signal virtues of the Blessed Martyr. There appeared in him something beyond expression, something more than human. The most savage hearts
were mollified at the sight of him. Even the most
timorous were in love with him. When he was carried out of the priests' yard for execution, he turned
towards our chamber windows, and with pleasant
aspect and elevated hand, he gave us his Bene-
diction."

Oliver Plunket teaches this same lesson of peace
and Catholic spirit even by the circumstances of the
disposition of his mangled body after his death.
His blessed head is prized by the people of
Drogheda, Ireland, and is preserved in the great
shrine there. But he is no less venerated in England
and particularly at the Benedictine Abbey at Down-
side. Foremost among those who pray constantly
for his canonization are the English monks at Down-
side, a curious, consoling and entirely Catholic
circumstance.

The Sons and Daughters of Patrick

The invincible meekness of characteristic Irish spirituality finds its inspiration in the words of Jesus: Amen, Amen, I say to you, unless the grain of wheat falling into the ground die, it remaineth alone. But if it die, it bringeth forth much fruit." It is taught in the line which sums up that school of Catholic asceticism which the Irish have always found so congenial: "If you wish to conquer, first learn to suffer." It is proclaimed in the phrase of St. Paul, a phrase which sums up at once the history and the spiritual portrait of St. Patrick's people: "Be not overcome by evil, but overcome evil by good!"

Another great priestly son of St. Patrick was Father Theobald Mathew, of the Nineteenth Century. The temperance movement that emanated from him brought before the world a man whose fame will live as long as the Irish race survives.

From 1838 onwards, it might be said, Father Mathew lived for the temperance movement. No words could convey the gigantic toil of these years. When almost every parish in Ireland was organized he crossed to England.

He spent himself entirely in the cause. Theobald Mathew was of that highly-strung temperment for which success itself brings dark moments of reaction. There is plenty of light and shade in his human life. By 1845 the Famine appeared and be-

gan to eat its way through the land into the hearts
of the people. During one of his journeys from Dublin to Cork the Apostle of Temperance saw the
people sitting on the fences bewailing bitterly the
destruction of everything around them. Temperance
was then almost forgotten for the moment by its
advocate. Back in Cork, we find him feeding the
hungry, hammering at the British Treasury with
suggestions and appeals for help, and trying to save
his people by the establishment of soup-shops from
the merciless profiteering of flour and corn mer-
chants. The trip to America in 1849, though it
aroused enthusiasm everywhere, was succeeded by
a sad return to a changed, inglorious Ireland.

All this is typically Irish: the moments of triumph, the tragic depths of defeat; the seeming outward disaster yet real inward glory; the constant
contradictions and reverses yet steady progress forward to perfection. These are the lessons taught by
the temperance crusade of Father Mathew. They
are typically Catholic lessons, yet completely Irish.

And Father Willie Doyle of our own century—
how Irish are the lessons of his life! Some one has
said that the Irish way of being Catholic might best
be described as the Way of the Cross. That Way
the Irish people learned from all their saints, beginning with St. Patrick. The distinctive mark of

those saints has always been austerity and heroic love of the Cross. Of this way, in our day, Father Willie Doyle is the example.

Father Willie Doyle wrote no books about suffering and expounded no theories about mystical love. But he has left us a little hint of the sufferings he cheerfully undertook out of love for Jesus. The story of his daily denials, kept a guarded secret from those around him, and still more the story of his self-inflicted sufferings, all to satisfy the love of his Crucified Master, which more and more devoured him, read like chapters from St. John of the Cross. "Last night I rose at twelve," he wrote in 1915, "and knelt in the cellar for an hour to suffer from the cold. It was a hard fight to do so, but Jesus helped me. I said my rosary with arms extended. At the third mystery the pain was so great that I felt I could not possibly continue; but at each Ave I prayed for strength and was able to finish it. This has given me great consolation by showing the many hard things I could do with the help of prayers." The many hard things, what a list they make! They are Father Doyle's "holy follies," the very exuberance of love which as a Kempis says, "often knows no measure but grows fervent beyond all measure." He would rise at midnight, tie his arms in the form of a cross and remain before the Blessed Sacrament in that position for three hours on end.

91

During the winter he used to slip out of the house in his night-shirt at 3 o'clock in the morning, and stand, up to his neck, in a frozen pond, praying for sinners.

You will say these things are excesses. No doubt they are, but they are Irish excesses, as any one knows who has been to St. Patrick's Purgatory or to the penitential islands of the truly Irish pilgrimages. The Irish way of being Catholic is the way of mortification, austerity and self-denial. Father William Doyle is the proof.

So is Matt Talbot. Matt is a model of Irish penance, self-discipline and spiritual heroism. But I mention him for another reason. He is also the typical Irish layman in the life of the Church.

As I have frequently pointed out, the unique thing in Irish Catholicism is the laity. Taken all through history the Irish priesthood has been magnificent; yet, Catholic priests tend to a certain magnificence wherever you find them: it is the occasional dimming of that magnificence, in a particular place at a particular time, that is exceptional, not its presence. But the thing that strikes every one who comes new to the vision of Catholic Ireland–the thing that lends the savor of miracle to the story of the Faith in Ireland–is the great nameless mass of the Irish faithful.

92

The strong and persistent feature in them is
their utter and fundamental religiousness–I do not
say holiness, for that varies from man to man, and
no nation is of necessity holier than another; but in
the Irish, even in the Irish sinner, there is this
"religiousness"–a supernatural awareness of God's
presence as something actual and obvious, a taking
for granted of the spiritual world.

No Irish layman has been canonized: till our
own day no Irish layman had even been thought of
for canonization. Bishops, abbots, nuns: but not
a layman. That, it may be, is the significance of
Matt Talbot. He may or may not come to be canonized: but saint or not he is a superb symbol–the ade-
quate and satisfying representative of that special
quality of Irish Catholicness. He has no meaning
save a religious meaning. Take away from him what
is Catholic and there is nothing left. He is totally
Catholic and his Catholicity is totally of the Irish
sort.

Thus the story of his life has no features save
religion. A simpler story cannot be imagined. He
was born in 1856 (and he who was so essentially
Irish in all things, was essentially Irish in this–that
he had a good mother). He went to work at twelve–
worked at a variety of jobs: he was a bricklayer's
laborer from the age of seventeen until at thirty-six

93

he became a laborer in a timber-yard and so remained until he died at sixty-nine. Nothing ever hap-
pened to him. He seems to have had no accidents;
nor, till the last couple of years, even an illness. He
wrote one letter in his life. He never went outside
Dublin. He never married, nor had he so much as a
love affair. No one man in a thousand has so event-
less a life, and when you find such a man, he is
usually pallid to watch, lifeless and featureless. But
this man was all strength and luminousness: the
natural life meant so little because the religious life
meant so much.

We all know the story of his drunkenness, his
repentance and his years of reformed virtue. That
is not the point about Matt Talbot. There is no looking at Matt Talbot without feeling that he is a perfect symbol of the Irish people at prayer: not one
sort of Irishman but the Irishman as such–the Irishman stripped down to his Catholicism.

Suffering and prayer have been the lot of Ireland for seven centuries: mixed with them have been
a score of other things, good and less good: but
those two steadily. And they have produced a
strongly marked type of Catholicism. Every one of
us knows the type–the Irishman in youth and middle
age regular in the practice of the Faith, developing
in old age into a life that is only prayer: at every

point of life marked by a certain decisiveness as of men who do not so much as see any alternative to faith. It is of this abiding type that Matt Talbot is the perfect representative. He is the essence of an Irishman: every Irishman smells a little of Matt Talbot unless he is lost altogether. And if Matt is canonized, a host of unknown Irishmen will be raised to the altars with him.

And what shall I say of Irish women? Every Irishman would wish me to name his mother in a catalogue of saintly Irish souls, and almost every one of them would be right. But the names of some Irish women deserve particular recollection here. Catherine McAuley is one, Mother McAuley of the Sisters of Mercy. Another is Nano Nagle, foundress of the Sisters of the Presentation; did ever a religious foundress have a name so typically Irish? Yet another is Mary Aikenhead, a girl from Cork who became a typical Irish woman at work in behalf of the Church. Some one once called her an Irish St. Teresa of Avila, and such she was both as a foundress and as a personality. So was Margaret Mary Hallahan, the great Dominican religious educator who had such good sense, such drive and such humility. She called herself "God's Broomstick"–and God used her well in His work of sweeping clean the ways of the world.

Such were the sons and daughters of Patrick. The extraordinary number of Irish saints in the earlier centuries witnesses to the dominant influence of the humble-hearted Patrick on the first generations. The subsequent history of Ireland makes it certain that the number of uncanonized saints, the holy men and the holy women whom the Church honors on the Feast of All Saints, is even more extraordinary.

The prayerfuless of St. Patrick was the virtue that made the Irish of all generations most like their patriarch. The monks and nuns of the early monasteries and the medieval abbeys centered the whole life around the altar and in the choir, making their primary occupation the "Praise of God." The persecuted generations sought courage and consolation in the furtive gatherings about the mass rock, assisting their soggarths in offering the Holy Sacrifice. They sustained themselves during the long forced absences of their hunted priests by telling Mary's beads over and over again in the secret prayers around their own fireplaces. Must they not have inspired one another with the vision of the slave boy fervently praying on the hills of Antrim? Again in the terrible years of the Black Famine when death stalked through their desolated land, and in the dreadful years when helplessly they watched the crowbar brigade batter down their humble cabins, they found their only comfort in the rosary of their heavenly Queen.

Those prayer-filled centuries of joy, and those prayer-filled centuries of agony have engraved deeply in the hearts of his modern children St. Patrick's heritage of prayer. When those of other nations, visiting Ireland, behold the devout throngs in the churches, when they listen to the steady murmur of the evening rosary in the homes, when they see the shrines that dot the land and the crosses that crown the mountain tops, when they watch the crowds climbing Croagh Patrick, praying at Lough Derg, or kneeling at Knock, they exclaim in loving admiration: "These are indeed a holy people." What more appreciative tribute could they pay to our prayerful patriarch?

The Irish Faith reaches below the surface and burns deeply into the heart. It is a way of life, not an outward garment that like a best suit is worn only on Sundays. You will meet a man on the road in Ireland who will tell you, "It's a soft day, thanks be to God," when it may be raining torrents and spoiling the hay and harvest that he is trying to save. But that doesn't matter. The rain is God's gift, so let it come down even in bucketfuls.

An Irish mother may lose her only child but she will tell you that God knew best and blessed be

His holy will. In those districts in Ireland where
the Gaelic tongue is spoken, they will salute you
with a prayer, "God bless you." And the answer is
equally beautiful, "God and Mary bless you." The
air in Ireland is charged with Faith and it springs
to lips in prayer at the slightest provocation.

I think God must sometimes smile when He
hears the Irish pray, for if He has a sense of humor,
and I am sure He has, He will give the Irish what
they ask for, if for no other reason than to save His
own good name.

They tell of a fisherwoman in Dublin who had
done her share to make Dublin a city of hospitality
for the thousands of pilgrims who thronged the
streets in the days of the International Eucharistic
Congress in 1932. Someone asked the fisherwoman
if she thought the threatening clouds were a sign of
rain. "Well," she says, "we have been praying for
fine weather for six months, and if it rains now God
has only Himself to blame." And it did not rain.

They still say the family Rosary in Ireland in
the evening, and to speak of that prayer to an Irish
exile is enough to stir up a host of memories–a family around the fireside bowed in prayer, the young-
sters in bare feet kneeling over the chairs, the dad
tired after his day in the fields, thumbing his beads
and missing the count of his decade, and the mother

who could pass for a queen, directing the wandering mind of her husband who is just as likely to say fifteen Hail Marys for his decade as he is to say ten.

Night after night, the ceremony was the same. Mother, dad, children—rosaries—the blazing turf fire. More perhaps than anything else, Ireland's devotion to Our Lady's Rosary has kept the Faith at white heat through all the centuries.

It was the quality of Christianity lived by Patrick and taught by him to the people that has ever brought God and the spiritual life so close to the Irish as to make them singular among all nations for the frankness, the simplicity and the beauty of their piety.

The humble practice of penance is also characteristic of the Irish as it is that of their saint. Someone once observed that the great shrines of the Latins are scenes of mingled piety and joy; that those of the Orientals are scenes of piety and awe; while those of the Irish are places of piety and penance. Lough Derg, St. Patrick's Purgatory, and the shrine of Our Lady of Knock are places of penitential discipline, humbly embraced by great multitudes in a typically Irish way, a way that those of other lands find almost superhuman and beyond belief.

Among the poor of Dublin, one sees that beneath the squalor, and in spite of it, there exists holiness of life and wonderful charity; holiness which reveals itself in the resignation with which the poor bear the manifold troubles that are their daily lot; charity which is seen in the kindness to those amongst them who are poorer than themselves. It is easy to be holy in the cloister or in the sheltered surroundings of a comfortable home, but to see real goodness go to a room in a tenement house of Ireland or into a little country cottage and look around you. There is the perpetual Lamp kept alive somehow, even though there is no bread. There are the objects of piety—crucifix, pictures, statues and the tiny altar decked in colored paper and tinsel. There a patient wife alone with her little ones, or the lonely widow with a smile of welcome.

Visit the churches on the night when the men's sodalities meet and see the thousands of workers of every class who, after their day's labor in yard or shop or tram, come week by week or month by month to gain new strength and help from their devotion to the practices of their sodality. Go on a Sunday morning to the early Masses and see the throngs of men and women who crowd the altar rails to receive their God and Master.

Follow the footsteps of the young men and the young women of the cities who visit the poor in their own homes, the wanderers in the lodging houses, the sick in the hospital wards. These are the people, the God-fearing people from whom a Matt Talbot sprang and who number amongst them many, who like Matt Talbot, live lives of holiness and self-sacrifice in the midst of their fellow-men.

It is to St. Patrick that we must trace all these characteristics of spirituality and of faith. As these qualities colored the nature of Patrick's sanctity, so these same qualities have given the Irish the specific differences among the nations of the earth. The green mantle of faith adorned with the fair flowers of prayer, penance and sacrifice that Patrick threw over Ireland, still covers it today.

To all lands came the missionaries of Christianity to reveal to their people that Christ was God—mighty in His poverty, powerful in His meekness, a conqueror on His Cross. In many instances they rejected the message or, having received it, they lost it by their attachment to worldly glory.

The same revelation came to Ireland through her apostle, Patrick, the same vision of the transitory values of the riches of the earth, of the eternal value of the Kingdom of God, but she fell into no like error. She recognized the Savior of men when He came to her, and ever since she has been faithful to Him. Her history, wretched in terms human, is one of ever-increasing triumph. Because of this, though old in sorrow and bitter experience, she is young in vigor of life and hope. Her spiritual and national survival she owes to her fidelity to Catholic ideals, and her history is that of generation after generation fighting valiantly to retain these ideals.

One of the proudest titles which Ireland claims is "Mother of Priests". From the days of St. Patrick, through the sixth to the ninth centuries when Irish monasteries sent forth their many sons to bring both faith and culture to a darkened Europe, on through 700 years of persecution when the faith was nourished from the Mass Rock high in the mountains, and down to our own generation Irish parents have sought no greater honor than to count a priest among their children.

Priests are an intimate part of Irish life. For it was the priests who sustained the people in their struggle for freedom. From the priest came the lessons which nurtured love of family, of country and of God.

Ireland nourished them with a rich and abiding faith; she filled their hearts with a wondrous hope; and for charity she gave them a love of Christ whose only seal could be and more than once was—martyrdom.

While Ireland was one of the last countries in Europe to receive the faith, she has never weakened but has grown in strength and good works. Ireland's chief export is the faith of St. Patrick. Her priests have been loved and reverenced in all the countries of the world and heroic tales of her laymen are told wherever there are Irish immigrants.

I recently read about a poor parish in County Mayo. But in God's sight it is very rich for it proudly claims 60 living priests on the foreign missions. Every year more than 400 priests are ordained in Ireland. Only 100 of these remain at home. A like number leave the country for dioceses in England, the United States, Australia and elsewhere. Another 75 go annually to the foreign missions of Asia and Africa while the remainder are ordained for the various religious orders. Ireland is proud to give these priestly sons to the Church in other lands and hundreds more of her sons and daughters to the Brotherhoods and Sisterhoods scattered throughout the world.

Today, just as in the past, the Irish know that God is near, no matter how dark the shadows may be. Joy and peace dwell in their hearts. From God's tabernacle home in every village and town and in busy Dublin this spirit of contentment flows out into the home, the fields and the factories and offices.

This sacramental presence of Christ gives the people a sense of joy and a sanity of outlook on life which the stranger cannot comprehend. They know that the Church is distinctly joyous in its sacraments, doctrines, and devotions, and in the number of its children who have been eminent for joy and wit and laughter in all ages.

Because of strong faith–the legacy of St. Patrick–God is present everywhere in Irish life. Most of all, He is in Irish hearts. There He lives and has His throne, a triumph of God's grace over generations who hand down their faith from father to son and from mother to daughter with the solemn words–"Keep it always alive!"

V

ST. PATRICK AND OUR DAY

St. Patrick and our Day

Almighty God in His mysterious wisdom permitted the Irish nation to be flung bleeding to the four corners of the earth. In a pitiful stream, the exiles crossed the waterways of the world, seeking that which was denied them at home. With them they brought their God and their Saint. As the banished Israelites, wandering in sorrow away from the Holy Land, clung to the Ark of the Covenant as the center of their life, so did the banished Irish, wandering in sorrow from their holy land, cling firmly to that of which the Ark of the Covenant was the symbol: the tabernacle wherein their God is enthroned. And fortified by the strength of nations, the exiles planted the Cross of Christ in Arctic ice and tropic sun, on the rolling prairies of America, amid the sands of Africa, by the mountains of Asia, and on the long, low plains of Australia.

The dispersion of the Irish is one of the wonders of God's Providence. We should never recall it to arouse bitterness–God forbid! We should look back to it as to one of the glories of the faith, just as we look back to the martyrs of the Roman arena, martyrs who saved both their own country and sometimes their oppressors by their fidelity. The marvelous results of this dispersion, one of the brightest pages in the history of Ireland and one of the grandest monuments to the undying vitality of the Church, are beyond computation. They are world-wide in extent and supernatural in power. Truly it is a case of God using the weak ones of the earth to confound the strong. We see a stream of broken-hearted, poverty-stricken exiles fleeing from their country. Yet look at the results. Strong with the strength of God, the poor exiles have built numberless monuments to their Creator—wayside churches, mighty cathedrals, seminaries, convents, orphanages and schools and foreign mission stations —all centers whence radiates the life of the grace of God, vivifying and uplifting every land.

If they have been faithful, it is because *Patrick* himself has been the source of their strength, the patron of their perseverance.

Nor is the power of Patrick far to seek; it is *Christ*—and Christ it must always be by whom the Irish and all others live, if their race or any race seeks to survive in glory.

It was in an era of alarming crisis that Pope Celestine I sent Patrick to Ireland—an era of confusion and disorder and chaos. Ours too are times of awesome crisis. Indeed one is guilty of no exaggeration in stating that never before in all history has Christian civilization been confronted with so dangerous and so diabolical an enemy as international Communism. For ultimately and essentially stakes at issue in the struggle that is being bitterly and pitilessly waged today by this vicious and satanic evil, are not merely lands or governments or riches or influence or power. The battle is for the souls of men.

St. Patrick and the Irish

If Christianity is to emerge victorious from this war, nothing is more desperately needed than the spirit of faith in the living God which permeated St. Patrick's own interior life.

In a new world, with new frontiers, with a new spirit of adventure, born of new conquests of nature, a new missionary spirit is needed in the Church. The divinely defined purposes of the Church's missionary endeavor are meeting the opposition of a world-wide movement which has arisen in a philosophy of life completely in contradiction with the truths upon which Christianity is founded.

We have been warned by the Soviets that our grandchildren will live under communist rule, whether we like it or not. Fifteen hundred years ago men were convinced that they were making history. Today the conviction is growing out of the new philosophy that history is making men, and that the efforts which we are making to change the course of the world are but part of a vast evolutionary process in which the world is engulfing us all into its own fatalistically determined changes.

Against this new and forboding outlook on life the Christian Church must continue to proclaim the eternal truths of the Gospel. Today as always the unity of the Church among all nations, the City of promise within the city of the world, is strengthened by the same Holy Spirit Who enkindled the fire of divine love in the souls of the Apostles on the first Pentecost. Today as always the unity of the Church finds external expression in the solidarity of all Christians under the Vicar of Christ within the city of this world.

In the days of Saint Patrick the Church was closely identified with all the political and social forces through which western civilization became articulate. Today, fifteen centuries after Patrick's death, the political power of the Church is confined within the limits of a tiny state, entirely destitute of the material forces which enable the nations of the world to struggle with one another for survival. The seed is the same which Patrick planted. The city of this world in which the seed is growing remains the same, despite the changes which have come over its visible structure. We must not be drawn by the prophets of the false philosophy which would surrender Christianity to the processes of a materialistically determined evolution.

We must go forth as Patrick did to meet the enemy. We must be supernaturally alive, as he was, with the conviction that, with Christ before us and behind us and around us, we cannot fail. At the same time, we must be willing, as Patrick was, to make the sacrifices by which the victory of Christianity in the city of this world may be won. Christ has sent us, as He sent Saint Patrick, not to be successful according to the standards of the world, but to be witnesses within the city of this world unto the truths of the City of God.

We must not aim to bring the world to Christ, with its false standards of success, its secularistic outlook on life and its narrowly conceived programs for freedom from want and insecurity. We must aim rather to bring Christ into the world, that the spirit of the world may be renewed according to the plan which His Heavenly Father outlined when His Divine Son was sent to become man for us and for our salvation. Our Blessed Lord has reminded us of the price which we must pay to be His disciples. He has told us that many of those to whom the Gospel is preached will refuse to receive it.

Despite failure and persecution, we must be witnesses of Christ, as was Patrick. We must not be discouraged when we are unable to defend the Church against hostile attack. We must not ourselves abandon the truth which Christ has taught us because so many who live only in the city of this world remain impervious to its influence.

111

St. Patrick and Our Day

Our modern age has a challenge of its own. It requires us to translate into our individual lives and into society as a whole the teachings of Christ; to attract others from a pursuit of material advantages to a reappraisal of the values and of the spiritual life; to transform society from the false teachings of Marx and Lenin to the gospel of Christ and the way of life which He taught; to convert Christians from worldliness to supernatural living. This challenge must be met by prayer, by knowledge, and especially by example so that those who are seeking Christ will find Him through the manner in which His gospel is clearly seen to affect the lives of those who profess it.

Today the world is searching for a link against a civilization so offensive to Christianity and Truth as to merit the term barbarian, in spite of its many artistic and scientific achievements. In economic and social life this link must join private ownership and individual initiative to a reconstructed industrialism. In political life it must seek contact with elements of strength unpolluted by totalitarian tyranny.

We cannot be sluggards in this age of turmoil. We cannot be apathetic. Let us face our own century with the courage with which St. Patrick faced

his distressing century fifteen hundred years ago
and repeat with him this prayer that came from the
depths of his apostolic soul:–

I arise today with a mighty strength, the invocation
   of the Trinity

     Through belief in the Threeness
     Through confession of the Oneness
        Toward the Creator
           and
May Thy Salvation, O Lord, be ever with us.
         Amen.

Daughters of St. Paul

IN MASSACHUSETTS
    50 St. Paul's Avenue, Boston, Ma. 02130
    172 Tremont Street, Boston, Ma. 02111
IN NEW YORK
    78 Fort Place, Staten Island, N.Y. 10301
    59 East 43rd Street, New York, N.Y. 10017
    625 East 187th Street, Bronx, N.Y. 10458
    525 Main Street, Buffalo, N.Y. 14203
IN NEW JERSEY
    Hudson Mall — Route 440 and
        Communipaw Avenue, Jersey City, N.J. 07304
IN CONNECTICUT
    202 Fairfield Avenue, Bridgeport, Ct. 06604
IN OHIO
    2105 Ontario St. (at Prospect Ave.), Cleveland,
        Oh. 44115
    25 E. Eighth Street, Cincinnati, Oh. 45202
IN PENNSYLVANIA
    1719 Chestnut Street, Philadelphia, Pa. 19103
IN FLORIDA
    2700 Biscayne Blvd., Miami, Fl. 33137
IN LOUISIANA
    4403 Veterans Memorial Blvd., Metairie, La. 70002
    1800 South Acadian Thruway, P.O. Box 2028,
        Baton Rouge, La. 70802
IN MISSOURI
    1001 Pine Street (at North 10th), St. Louis, Mo. 63101
IN TEXAS
    114 East Main Plaza, San Antonio, Tx. 78205
IN CALIFORNIA
    1570 Fifth Avenue, San Diego, Ca. 92101
    46 Geary Street, San Francisco, Ca. 94108
IN HAWAII
    1143 Bishop Street, Honolulu, Hi. 96813
IN ALASKA
    750 West 5th Avenue, Anchorage, Ak. 99501
IN CANADA
    3022 Dufferin Street, Toronto 395, Ontario, Canada
IN ENGLAND
    57, Kensington Church Street, London W. 8, England
IN AUSTRALIA
    58 Abbotsford Rd., Homebush, N.S.W., Sydney 2140,
    Australia